INSECTS

J EN G REEN

Gareth Stevens Publishing
MILWAUKEE

The original publishers would like to thank the following children, and their parents, for modeling in this book — Rodney Ammah, Dolly Batkhismig, Joshua Cooper, Charlene Da-Cova, Rachel Greiner, Ion Kojokari, Armani McKenzie, Alejandro Otalvora, Sussy Quirke, and Mark Stafford. The publishers also thank Sarah Wood.

Gareth Stevens Publishing would like to extend special thanks to Dr. Gerald Noonan for his expert assistance in verifying the accuracy of this text. Dr. Noonan is Curator of Insects at the Milwaukee Public Museum. His research interests include studying the evolution, classification, and biogeography of carabid beetles.

**For a free color catalog describing Gareth Stevens'
list of high-quality books and multimedia programs,
call 1-800-542-2595 (USA) or 1-800-461-9120 (Canada).
Gareth Stevens Publishing's Fax: (414) 225-0377.**

Library of Congress Cataloging-in-Publication Data

Green, Jen.
Insects / by Jen Green.
p. cm. — (Young scientist concepts and projects)
Includes bibliographical references and index.
Summary: Describes different kinds of insects and their behavior.
Includes fact boxes and suggested activities and projects.
ISBN 0-8368-2266-8 (lib. bdg.)
1. Insects—Juvenile literature. 2. Insects—Experiments—
Juvenile literature. [1. Insects. 2. Insects—Experiments.
3. Experiments.] I. Title. II. Series.
QL467.2.G735 1999
595.7—dc21 98-34715

This North American edition first published in 1999 by
Gareth Stevens Publishing
1555 North RiverCenter Drive, Suite 201
Milwaukee, WI 53212 USA

Original edition © 1998 by Anness Publishing Limited.
First published in 1998 by Lorenz Books, an imprint of
Anness Publishing Inc., New York, New York.
This U.S. edition © 1999 by Gareth Stevens, Inc.
Additional end matter © 1999 by Gareth Stevens, Inc.

Project editor: Sophie Warne
Text editor: Charlotte Evans
Consultant: Michael Chinery
Children's photographer: John Freeman
Nature photographer: Robert Pickett
Stylist: Melanie Williams
Designer: Caroline Grimshaw
Illustrator: Alan Male
Gareth Stevens series editor: Dorothy L. Gibbs
Editorial assistant: Diane Laska

Printed in the United States of America

1 2 3 4 5 6 7 8 9 03 02 01 00 99

YOUNG SCIENTIST CONCEPTS & PROJECTS

INSECTS

CONTENTS

INCREDIBLE INSECTS

Swallowtail butterfly

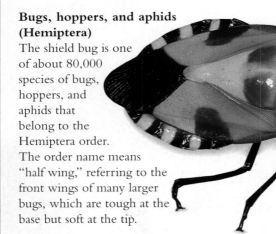

Butterflies and moths (Lepidoptera)

The swallowtail butterfly belongs to the Lepidoptera order, which has about 150,000 species. The order name means "scale wings." The wings of butterflies and moths are covered with tiny scales that overlap like roof tiles.

Bugs, hoppers, and aphids (Hemiptera)

The shield bug is one of about 80,000 species of bugs, hoppers, and aphids that belong to the Hemiptera order. The order name means "half wing," referring to the front wings of many larger bugs, which are tough at the base but soft at the tip.

Shield bug

INSECTS make up three-quarters of all animal species in the world. More than a million insect species are known, with many more still to be discovered. They are found in steamy rain forests, on top of mountains, and in the middle of barren deserts. A few kinds are harmful, spreading disease and damaging crops or buildings. Many more, however, are helpful. They pollinate plants and fertilize the soil. As many as ten thousand insects can live on a single square yard (square meter) of Earth's surface, making them an important food source for many animals. Insects are invertebrates, which means that, unlike birds, reptiles, and mammals, they do not have a backbone. Insects have three pairs of legs, and most adult insects have one or two pairs of wings. To help identify insects, experts classify them into "orders." Most orders contain many thousands of species. All the species in one order have similar life cycles and share certain features, such as the shape of their wings or mouthparts. Some of the orders with the most species are shown on these two pages.

Greenbottle fly

Flies (Diptera)

There are about 100,000 species in the Diptera order, including the greenbottle fly. *Diptera* means "two wings." Flies have only one pair of wings. Instead of rear wings, they have tiny balancing organs, called halteres.

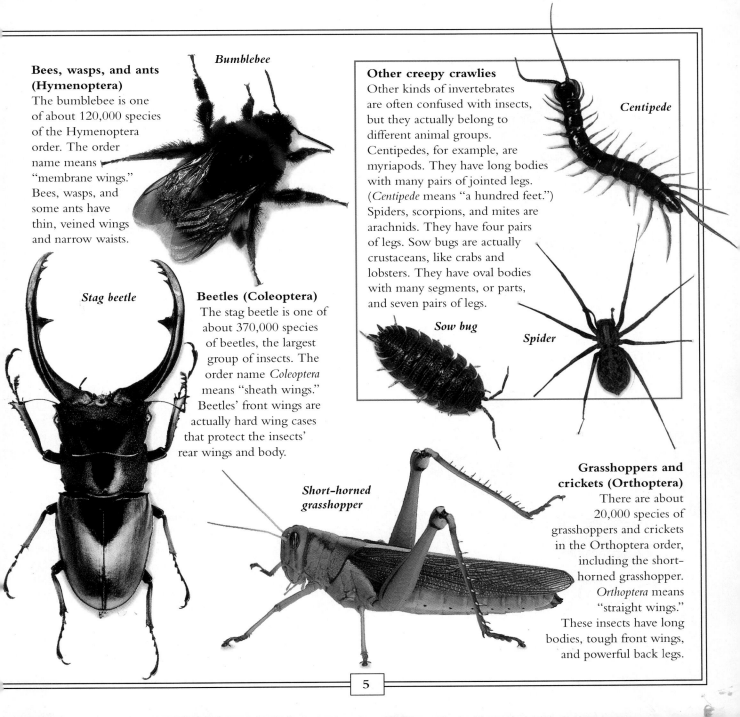

Bees, wasps, and ants (Hymenoptera)

The bumblebee is one of about 120,000 species of the Hymenoptera order. The order name means "membrane wings." Bees, wasps, and some ants have thin, veined wings and narrow waists.

Bumblebee

Other creepy crawlies

Other kinds of invertebrates are often confused with insects, but they actually belong to different animal groups. Centipedes, for example, are myriapods. They have long bodies with many pairs of jointed legs. (*Centipede* means "a hundred feet.") Spiders, scorpions, and mites are arachnids. They have four pairs of legs. Sow bugs are actually crustaceans, like crabs and lobsters. They have oval bodies with many segments, or parts, and seven pairs of legs.

Centipede

Sow bug

Spider

Beetles (Coleoptera)

The stag beetle is one of about 370,000 species of beetles, the largest group of insects. The order name *Coleoptera* means "sheath wings." Beetles' front wings are actually hard wing cases that protect the insects' rear wings and body.

Stag beetle

Grasshoppers and crickets (Orthoptera)

There are about 20,000 species of grasshoppers and crickets in the Orthoptera order, including the short-horned grasshopper. *Orthoptera* means "straight wings." These insects have long bodies, tough front wings, and powerful back legs.

Short-horned grasshopper

LOOKING FOR INSECTS

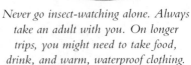

INSECTS are easy to find; they are everywhere. A good place to start looking is in a local park — or your own garden. You will find an amazing variety. An average city garden might have up to three hundred species of beetles, with as many kinds of moths and several different butterflies. That same small area could contain up to two hundred kinds of flies, ninety different bugs, and many species of bees, ants, and wasps. Different types of insects live and feed in long grasses, in flower beds and hedges, under logs and stones, and in the soil. Do a survey to find out which species prefer these different habitats, or homes. Mark off study areas at four different sites and see how many insect species you can find at each site. Remember to replace any stones and logs you turn over and try not to damage any plants.

Never go insect-watching alone. Always take an adult with you. On longer trips, you might need to take food, drink, and warm, waterproof clothing.

Collecting jar with magnifying lid

Backpack

Piece of cheesecloth secured with a rubber band

Clean jar

Collecting jar

Magnifying glass

Field guide

Camera

Soft paintbrush (for picking up insects)

Ruler

Gloves

Notebook

Pencils

Colored pencils

Insect-watching equipment
The equipment shown here will help you study insects, but you do not need all of it to start. A magnifying glass and a collecting jar are often enough. Record what you find in a notebook and use a field guide to help you identify the different species.

Insect survey

1 Wearing gloves, use tent stakes and string to mark off a square yard (sq m) in an area of long grass. Measure 3 feet (1 m) on each side.

2 What insects do you find inside the square? Use a collecting jar and a magnifying glass to study them. Record what you find in a notebook.

3 Mark off another square yard (sq m) in an area with flowers or a hedge. You might find aphids and ladybugs on plant stems and leaves.

MATERIALS

You will need: gardening gloves, 4 tent stakes, string, tape measure, collecting jar, magnifying glass, pencil, notebook, field guide, colored pencils.

6 Use a field guide to identify the insects you find. How many species were in each area? Draw a chart to show your survey results.

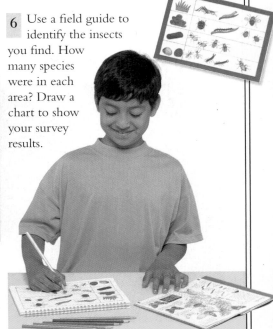

4 Move a fallen log to see the kinds of insects that live underneath it. Be sure you wear gloves to protect your hands. You might find beetles under logs and earwigs under bark.

5 Still wearing gloves, carefully look under some rocks. What kinds of insects prefer this habitat? You might find ground beetles or an ants' nest.

WHAT IS AN INSECT?

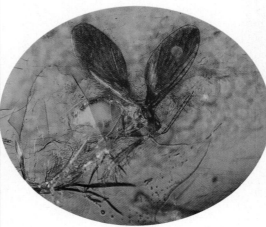

Inside this piece of amber (above) *is a fossil fly. Amber is fossilized sap from pine trees that grew millions of years ago. The fly was trapped in the sticky sap and preserved as the sap hardened into amber.*

Birds, reptiles, and mammals all have internal skeletons to provide a framework for their bodies. Insects are different — they have their skeletons on the outside. Their soft body parts are protected by a hard case, called an exoskeleton, made of a tough, light material called chitin. Chitin forms a waterproof barrier around the insect that keeps it from drying out and also prevents air from passing through it. Tiny holes, called spiracles, along each side of the insect's body let air inside. Unlike birds or mammals, insects are cold-blooded animals, which means that the temperature of an insect's body is about the same as its surroundings. To warm up, an insect basks in the sunshine. When it gets too hot, it moves into the shade. In very cold weather, insects find it difficult to move at all. Many adult insects die in winter. Others enter a deep sleep, called hibernation, and wake up again in the spring.

Insect fossils
Insects are a very ancient group of animals, as this 130-million-year-old dragonfly fossil *(left)* shows. Insects have lived on Earth for over 400 million years. They were the first animals to fly 350 million years ago. Many of the species we know today developed about 100 million years ago, when flowering plants first appeared.

Modern insects
A modern dragonfly *(above)* looks very similar to its prehistoric ancestor. Most of the earliest insect species, however, are now extinct.

Three sections

The bodies of all adult insects have three main sections — head, thorax, and abdomen. Each section is made up of small plates that fit together at flexible joints. The head has mouthparts, antennae, and eyes. Legs and wings are attached to the thorax. The abdomen contains the reproductive organs and part of the digestive system.

Wasp

Antenna

Head

Eye

Jointed leg

Thorax

Exoskeleton

Wing

Abdomen

Body systems

An insect's internal systems are protected by its hard exoskeleton. This diagram (below) separates the main systems, which are color coded to make them clearly visible. The nervous system (purple) relays messages from the senses to the brain. In the respiratory system (gray), air enters the body through spiracles and is carried through tiny pipes, called tracheae, to other parts of the body. In the circulatory system (red), several hearts, arranged in a row, pump blood around the body. The digestive system (green, orange) processes food in the gut. Special tubes filter waste and expel it through the anus.

Simple brain

Trachea

Heart

Waste filters

Anus

Main nerve

Gut

Spiracle

FACT BOX

• Insects are a very successful animal group. Because they are small, they can live in small places and survive on very little food.

• Giant dragonflies flew in hot, humid forests 350 million years ago. Fossilized remains of these early insects are found in rocks.

• Cockroaches belong to a group of very ancient insects. Fossils show their ancestors were around 300 million years ago.

Young insects

This puss moth caterpillar is a young insect. Its body has many segments. Each segment has a pair of spiracles, which look like tiny portholes. Many insects change shape dramatically as they grow into adults.

Segment

Spiracle

Puss moth caterpillar

RECORDING INSECTS

Whe studying insects, your notebook is an important piece of equipment. You will use it to record a variety of information about all the insects you see. When you see an insect, write down the date, time, and weather conditions and describe the location where the insect was found. You could even draw a map to show the location. Make sketches of insects in your notebook, too. Whenever possible, study the insects you see by looking at them through a magnifying glass. Notice the shape of the insect's body. Is it short and rounded, or long and slender? Does the insect have wings? How many? What do they look like? Does the insect have hard wing cases? Look at the insect's legs. Are they long or short? Can you see the joints? Can you tell the difference between legs used for digging or swimming or jumping? Study the insect's mouthparts and antennae. Are the mouthparts for chewing or for sucking? What do the antennae look like? Your notes and sketches can be rough at first. You can redo them neatly later. If you have a spiral-bound notebook, you can tear out pages and keep all the notes you make about a particular insect together.

Collecting insects
Butterflies, like most other insects, are fragile. They can be difficult to pick up and examine without harming them. A collecting jar can help you safely gather insects to study.

Drawing insects
As you study insects, you can make sketches in your notebook to help you remember exactly what they looked like. Use a field guide to help you find out the species of each insect and to what order or family each one belongs. This project shows you, step by step, how to make drawing insects a little easier.

Drawing insects

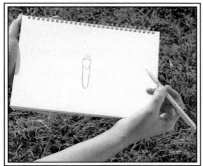

You will need: magnifying glass, pencil, notebook, colored pencils.

1 Study an insect closely through a magnifying glass. Use a pencil to draw an outline of the insect in your notebook. Start by drawing three ovals to show the three main parts of the insect's body — head, thorax, and abdomen.

2 Draw in the details of the insect's head — antennae, eyes, and mouthparts. Draw in the legs and outline the wings attached to the thorax. If the insect's wings are folded, it might be more difficult to see how they are attached.

WARNING
Always be sure to return the insects you collect, unharmed, to the places where you found them.

3 Finally, draw in any markings and important or unusual features you can see on the insect's body or wings, such as the distinctive eyespots on this butterfly's back wings. Complete your drawing by coloring it in as accurately as you can. You can leave the drawing in your notebook or mount it on colored paper to display. Be sure to label your drawing with the name of the insect. Use a field guide to help you find the insect's species and order and add those names to the drawing, too.

SEEING AND HEARING

THE world is a dangerous place for an insect. Many enemies are just waiting to kill it and eat it. To survive, an insect must find food and escape its enemies. It relies on its senses of sight, hearing, touch, taste, and smell for help, but insect senses are not the same as human senses. To see, most species have three simple eyes, called ocelli. The ocelli are light-sensitive and can tell light from dark. Insects also have large compound eyes that have many lenses. Their compound eyes help insects see fine details, even in the dark. They can see colors, and they also see ultraviolet light, so they can use the sun to navigate, even in cloudy weather. To hear, insects sense sound vibrations with their eardrums. Most insects' ears, however, are not found on their heads. The praying mantis, for example, has ears on its thorax, between its hind legs.

Compound eyes
Compound eyes have many lenses. A dragonfly (*above*) has the largest eyes of any insect, with up to 30,000 lenses on each eye. Bees have about 5,000 lenses, but some ants have only nine.

Hexagonal lens

Optic nerve

Conical lens

Nerve fibers

This diagram (above) shows a cross section of a compound eye. The surface of the eye has tiny hexagonal (six-sided) lenses that fit together. Below them are conical lenses that focus light onto nerve fibers that carry signals to the brain via the optic nerve.

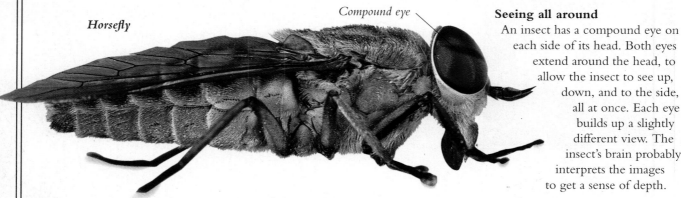

Horsefly

Compound eye

Seeing all around
An insect has a compound eye on each side of its head. Both eyes extend around the head, to allow the insect to see up, down, and to the side, all at once. Each eye builds up a slightly different view. The insect's brain probably interprets the images to get a sense of depth.

Insect eyes

Insect vision is very different from human vision. Experts think that each lens of an insect's compound eye sees a small part of a scene, giving the insect a mosaiclike view that builds into a bigger picture. These diagrams *(right)* compare how a human sees a moving insect and what experts think an insect sees. Because an insect has many more lenses, it can sense tiny movements human eyes would hardly notice. An insect will be more sensitive than a human to a bee taking off because a different set of lenses is affected.

Human vision *Insect vision*

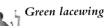

Green lacewing

Insect ears

Insects' eardrums are thin membranes of skin that vibrate from sounds, sending signals to the brain. Insects' ears are found in various places. The green lacewing hears with sensitive hairs on its wings. A grasshopper has ears on its abdomen. A cricket's ears are on its front legs, just below the knee.

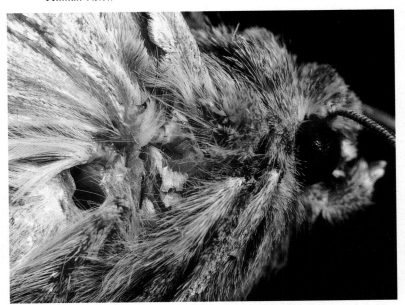

This noctuid moth (above) has its wings raised, clearly showing an ear hole on the side of its thorax. The moth can hear the high-pitched squeak of a hunting bat, so it can escape an attack. That squeak is far too high for human ears to hear.

TOUCH, TASTE, AND SMELL

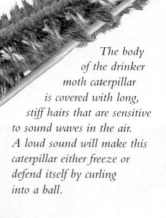

Aɴ insect's main sense organs are its antennae. These projections are covered with tiny hairs that are sensitive to touch, but they can do much more than feel. Many insects use their antennae to taste and smell — and even to hear. Smell is the most important sense for many insects. Some moths have long, feathery antennae that are sensitive to smell. Insects' antennae can also be sensitive to dampness and heat. Body lice use their antennae to measure moisture in the air, then use that information to seek out the damp parts of humans, where they make their homes. The antennae of blood-sucking insects act as heat detectors to sense the body heat of the warm-blooded animals on which these insects feed. Some insects have taste organs on their mouthparts. In many species, however, taste organs are located on the feet. Insects' bodies are covered with tiny, sensitive hairs that detect vibrations in the air to help the insects know which way is up and how fast they are flying.

The body of the drinker moth caterpillar is covered with long, stiff hairs that are sensitive to sound waves in the air. A loud sound will make this caterpillar either freeze or defend itself by curling into a ball.

Weevil

Cockroach

Antenna

Weevils have antennae branching from their snouts. The tips of the antennae are covered with sensitive hairs. The weevil has biting jaws on the end of its snout.

Cerci
Cockroaches and some crickets have special bristles, called cerci, on their abdomens with which they can sense vibrations in the air caused by noise or movement. The slightest hint of danger will send the cockroach scurrying for cover.

Cerci

Tasty feet
The housefly has taste sensors on its feet. As soon as it lands, it begins to suck up its liquid food through spongy mouthparts.

Honeybee

Antenna

Reacting to senses
The honeybee's sense organs are connected to nerve cells that send signals to its brain. Like other insects, the honeybee cannot think. It reacts instinctively to messages from the senses, which give the signal to feed, mate, or fly away.

Compound eye

Housefly

Antenna

Branching antennae
The antennae of the cockchafer beetle have many branches. The beetle spreads out this array of sensors like a fan to smell the wind and sense vibrations in the air.

Cockchafer beetle

REPRODUCTION

For any insect species to survive, its members must reproduce. Almost all insects reproduce by laying eggs. Most mate before the female lays her eggs. The sexes attract one another by sending special courtship signals. Some communicate by smell; others use special sounds or visual signals. Male stag beetles, for example, have huge jaws shaped like stags' antlers, which are used for fighting with other males to attract females. A female silk moth attracts a male moth by producing a special scent, called a pheromone. The male moth can smell the scent from several miles (kilometers) away and follows it to find the female. After mating, many insects lay their eggs on plants that will provide food for the young when they hatch. Other species lay their eggs in water, on the soil, or underground. After laying eggs, most insects fly away and take no further care of their young.

This grasshopper (above) is scraping its hind legs against its front wings. Rows of tiny pegs on the hind legs produce a harsh, chirping sound. Male grasshoppers make this noise to attract females — and to warn other males away. Crickets make a similar sound by rubbing the rough edges of their wings together.

Stag beetles

Battling beetles

Male stag beetles battle with each other for the chance to mate with a female. The males of this species have huge, antlerlike jaws, which they use for wrestling. They wrestle to advertise themselves to the females when they are ready to mate. Using its powerful jaws, a male stag beetle grabs a rival and lifts it into the air. Then it throws the opponent to the ground. The females of the species judge the males on how successful they are in this competition.

Fast breeders

Some species of insects can reproduce without mating or even laying eggs. In spring, female aphids *(left)* give birth to live young that are miniature versions of themselves. The young aphids begin to feed immediately and can reproduce themselves when only a week old.

Mating beetles

A male and female lily beetle mate on a plant stem. In this species, mating takes several hours. A complicated courtship helps the female make sure she has chosen a good mate. In other insects, mating takes only a few minutes.

Lily beetles

Caring for their young

Unlike most species of insects, female earwigs stay to guard their eggs and look after their young. The female earwig guards her eggs in an underground burrow. She licks the eggs clean and keeps them warm. When they hatch, she protects the young for several days and feeds them with food from her own stomach.

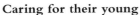

Heart shapes

When a pair of damselflies *(left)* mates, the male grasps the female's neck using claspers on the tip of his abdomen. The female arches her body up to collect sperm from the male to fertilize her eggs. As they mate, damselflies make the shape of a heart, and they can fly along in this position while they are mating.

LIFE CYCLES

Wᴴᴇɴ insects hatch from their eggs, they are ravenous. Most young insects consume huge quantities of food and grow quickly. Like their parents, their bodies are protected by a tough exoskeleton. As they grow, they must molt, or shed, this body case and grow a new one. As they molt, the young insects change shape, until they reach adulthood. This changing process is called metamorphosis. In some species of insects, the changes happen gradually. For example, young grasshoppers and dragonflies, called nymphs, look like their parents, except that they have no wings. They change gradually as they grow, until they become mature. In other species, changes happen suddenly. Some young insects, called larvae, look nothing like their parents. Their bodies must pass through a number of dramatic changes before they become adults. Caterpillars and grubs are larvae.

Red admiral butterfly

Different kinds of insects spend varying amounts of time in their young and adult forms. The red admiral butterfly spends five weeks as a caterpillar, two weeks as a pupa, and nine months as an adult. Mayflies, however, spend up to three years as nymphs, but only a few hours as adults.

Incomplete metamorphosis
Newly hatched mantis nymphs (*left*) look like their parents but have no wings. As they grow, they will molt, or shed, their outgrown skins. Their wings will develop gradually from wing buds. With each molt, the young insects will become more like the adults (*right*), finally emerging from the last molt complete with wings and reproductive organs. This gradual change is called incomplete metamorphosis.

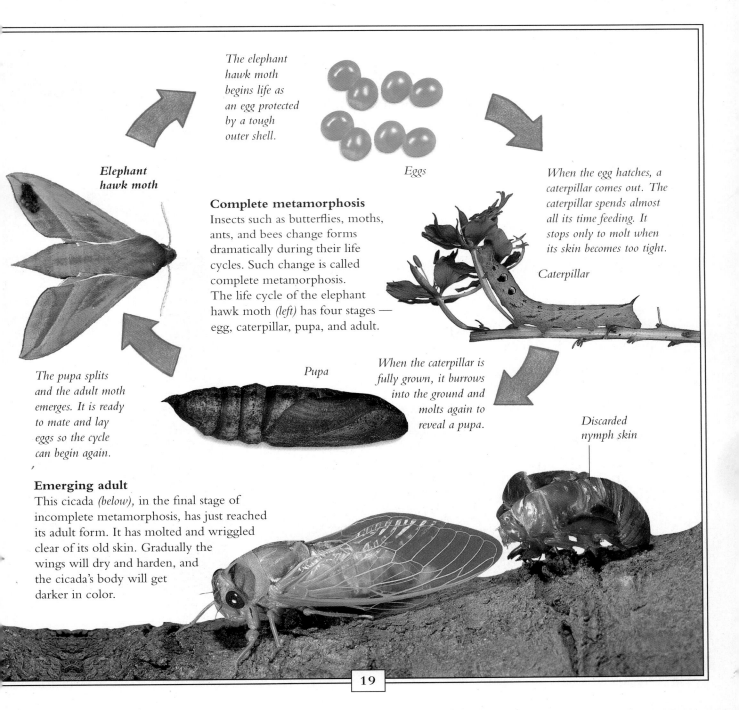

The elephant hawk moth begins life as an egg protected by a tough outer shell.

Eggs

Elephant hawk moth

When the egg hatches, a caterpillar comes out. The caterpillar spends almost all its time feeding. It stops only to molt when its skin becomes too tight.

Caterpillar

Complete metamorphosis

Insects such as butterflies, moths, ants, and bees change forms dramatically during their life cycles. Such change is called complete metamorphosis. The life cycle of the elephant hawk moth *(left)* has four stages — egg, caterpillar, pupa, and adult.

Pupa

When the caterpillar is fully grown, it burrows into the ground and molts again to reveal a pupa.

The pupa splits and the adult moth emerges. It is ready to mate and lay eggs so the cycle can begin again.

Discarded nymph skin

Emerging adult

This cicada *(below),* in the final stage of incomplete metamorphosis, has just reached its adult form. It has molted and wriggled clear of its old skin. Gradually the wings will dry and harden, and the cicada's body will get darker in color.

STUDYING LIFE CYCLES

Y OU can learn a lot about the life cycles of moths and butterflies by keeping caterpillars. First, prepare a home for the caterpillars using a cardboard box. Look for caterpillars on plants where you see half–eaten leaves and stems. You might find them hiding on the undersides of leaves. Make careful notes about the plants on which you found the caterpillars and take some leaves with you. As a caterpillar, the small tortoiseshell butterfly *(right)* feeds on stinging nettles. Use a field guide to identify the species you find and the kinds of plants they prefer. When picking up caterpillars, try not to touch them directly with your fingers; some species have hairs that will sting you. Instead, pick them up with a paintbrush or get them to climb onto a leaf. Carry them home in a collecting jar. At home, keep them in a box in a moist, cool place and out of direct sunlight. Clean the box regularly, replacing old leaves with fresh ones, and try to disturb the caterpillars as little as possible.

When your caterpillars become adult moths or butterflies, it is time to let them go. Take the insects back to where you found them. Lift the lid off their box and let them fly away.

M A T E R I A L S

You will need: scissors, cardboard box, strong tape, cheesecloth or netting, modeling clay, rubber gloves, fresh leaves, paper towels, collecting jar, ruler, pencil, notebook, field guide, colored pencils.

Keeping caterpillars

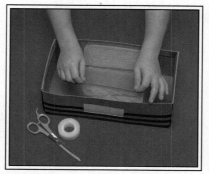

1 Cut window holes in the long sides of a box. Use strong tape to attach pieces of cheesecloth or netting over the windows to cover them.

2 Cut a piece of cheesecloth or netting for a lid, weighing down the corners with modeling clay to keep the caterpillars from escaping.

3 Wear rubber gloves to put leaves in the box. Provide fresh leaves daily and be sure the leaves are from a plant your caterpillars eat.

4 Put damp paper towels in a corner of the box to provide moisture. Carefully transfer the caterpillars from the collecting jar to the box and cover the box with the cheesecloth lid. Check the caterpillars and replace the damp paper towels every day. Keep daily notes about how much the caterpillars eat and how big they are.

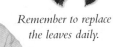

Remember to replace the leaves daily.

5 Watch how the caterpillars feed and move around. Record the dates when you see them molting. How many times did they shed their skins?

Chart the life cycles of your insects.

June–July	caterpillar feeds
end July	pupa forms
mid–August	butterfly emerges

6 When they finish growing, caterpillars attach themselves to twigs, spin a chrysalis or cocoon, and change into pupae. Add a twig to your box for this stage.

7 Check each pupa every day and write down the date when you see the case splitting. How long did each insect spend as a pupa?

8 You will see a butterfly or a moth struggle out of its chrysalis or cocoon. Before flying, it pumps blood into its crumpled wings to straighten them.

GETTING AROUND

Egyptian grasshopper

Coxa

Femur

Joint

Tibia

Tarsus

When it is about to jump, a grasshopper gathers its long legs under its body. The leg muscles contract, straightening the leg and pushing the insect upward.

Insects have six jointed legs for getting around. All insects' legs have the same basic structure. They are like hollow tubes. Each leg is joined to the insect's thorax by the coxa. The femur and tibia are like your thigh and lower leg. The tarsus corresponds to your foot and has two claws. All the sections meet at flexible joints. Muscles inside the leg expand (lengthen) and contract (shorten) to make it move. Different species move in different ways. The way they move helps identify them. The shape of an insect's legs depends on how it moves around its particular habitat. Insects that walk or run have long, thin legs. Those that jump, such as crickets, have powerful back legs. A few species have strong front legs for digging. Some insects that live in water have wide, flat back legs covered with long hairs. The back legs move together and act like oars to row the insect through the water.

Champion jumpers

Fleas are biting insects that feed on the blood of other animals. These small insects are amazing jumpers. They have very powerful back legs to help them leap onto the bodies of much larger animals. They can leap up to a foot (30 centimeters) in the air — 130 times their own height.

Flea

A springtail (above), like a flea, can jump into the air. Unlike a flea, however, a springtail uses its forked tail, rather than its legs, to jump. The tail is folded beneath the springtail's body. When it flicks down against the ground, the insect's body is thrown forward.

Housefly

Legs for digging

The mole cricket *(right)*, like a real mole, has strong, shovel–like front legs. This unusual insect spends its life underground. Its front legs shovel earth aside as the cricket tunnels through soil looking for underground roots to eat. It has special, scissorlike mouthparts for feeding.

Walking upside down

Houseflies and bluebottles have sucker pads and hooks on the soles of their feet that help them crawl up smooth surfaces, such as walls and windows. They can even walk across the ceiling upside down.

A looper caterpillar, or inchworm, has two pairs of claspers on the back end of its body. The caterpillar moves by bringing its claspers forward, arching its body into a loop. Then it stretches its front legs forward to move on.

Hawk moth caterpillar

Looper caterpillar

Clasper

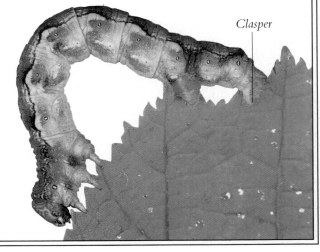

Caterpillar movements

Caterpillars have three pairs of true legs and several pairs of false legs. You can see the true legs of this hawk moth caterpillar at the front (left side) of its long body. It has five pairs of false legs, called prolegs, at the rear. Prolegs are muscular, suckerlike projections. The caterpillar moves only one pair of legs at a time to distribute its weight evenly along its body and to help it move over obstacles.

FRESHWATER INSECTS

MANY kinds of insects are found in fresh water. Some live in large lakes, rivers, or marshes. Others inhabit small ponds and shallow streams — or even puddles. Freshwater insects include many kinds of bugs and beetles. Most are predators and feed on small creatures that fall into the water. Some insects spend only the early part of their lives in water. As nymphs or larvae, they take advantage of the abundant food supply found there to feed on and help them grow. When these young insects become adults, they live on land. Like other animals, freshwater insects need air to breathe. Some have developed tubes and gills to help them breathe underwater.

Walking on water

The water strider *(above)* has long, thin legs and a lightweight body to help it walk on water. It spreads out its legs and skims along the surface. A "skin" on the surface of the water keeps the insect from sinking. The water strider moves along by rowing with its back and middle legs.

The water boatman, or back swimmer (above), swims upside down beneath the water's surface. Its hind legs are like oars rowing the insect along. When it senses vibrations made by another creature, it rushes over to stab the victim and drink its juices.

Breathing underwater

The water scorpion *(left)* has a tube at the end of its abdomen. When it needs to breathe, it raises the tube to the surface of the water like a snorkel. The tube is fringed with hairs so water cannot get inside.

The water beetle (left) traps a bubble of air under its wings before it dives. When it swims underwater, it uses this bubble as an air supply, just like a diver uses an oxygen tank. The beetle has to swim strongly so it does not bob back up to the surface.

Watery home

The larva of the caddis fly (*left*) lives underwater. It spins itself a protective case of silk. To keep its home well hidden, the larva attaches small sticks and stones from the pond or streambed to the outside of the case.

From water to land

The damselfly spends its early life as a nymph living underwater. It has three feathery gills on the tip of its abdomen to filter oxygen from the water to breathe. When the nymph is fully grown, it uses a plant stem to climb out of the water (*left*). Its skin splits, and a young adult appears. The young adult damselfly (*right*) rests after it emerges. Its abdomen and thorax lengthen as the insect stretches its crumpled wings. When the wings are dry, the damselfly takes to the air for the first time.

WATCHING POND INSECTS

You will need:
gardening gloves,
trowel, dishpan,
gravel, water
plants, large stones,
watering can.

YOU will find many kinds of freshwater insects in a pond or a stream. Spring and summer are good times to look for them because young insects turn into adults during these seasons. You can make a small pool for insects in your garden or perhaps at school. Be sure to ask a responsible adult for permission to dig the pool. To catch water insects to study, you will need a net, which you can make yourself. When you go to catch insects at the pond, take an adult with you for safety. As you approach the water, move quietly, or you will disturb the wildlife. Never run near water — you could easily trip and fall in. Different insects live in various places in a pond or a stream. Some live near the surface; others swim at the bottom. Lift up stones and pebbles to find the creatures that lurk on the undersides. Record the date, time, and place where you found the insects. Visit different ponds and streams, if possible, to see how the species you find vary.

Make an insect pool

1 Wear gloves when you make an insect pool. Dig a hole in the ground with a trowel. Make the hole big enough to fit a dishpan inside it.

2 Place a dishpan in the hole and press it down firmly. Cover the bottom of the pan with gravel and put in some water plants. Arrange stones inside and around the edge.

3 Use a watering can to fill the dishpan with water. When the pool is finished, insects and other animal life will quickly be attracted to it.

Make a pond net

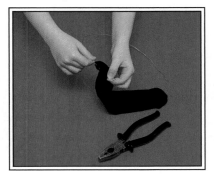

1 Thread wire in and out around the top of a thin stocking. You might need pliers to bend the wire into a circle.

2 Use pliers to twist the ends of the wire together to make the net secure. Then position the net at the end of a long pole.

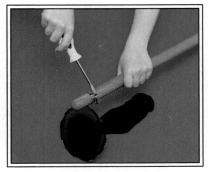

3 Slide the hose clamp over the pole and push the twisted wires under the clamp. Tighten the clamp with a screwdriver.

4 Capture insects by sweeping the net gently through the water. Lightly tap the stems of plants to knock other insects into the net.

MATERIALS

You will need: wire, thin stocking, pliers, long pole or broom handle, hose clamp, screwdriver, pitcher, empty plastic container, magnifying glass, field guide.

5 Pour a pitcherful of pond water into a plastic container. Then carefully empty your net into the water. Observe the insects and other creatures in the water through a magnifying glass. Use a field guide to help identify them. Take the creatures back to the pond when you have finished studying them.

INSECTS IN FLIGHT

Like all flies, the cranefly (above) has only one pair of wings. Instead of rear wings, it has tiny balancing organs, called halteres, to help it maneuver in the air. Halteres look like little knobs on stalks.

INSECTS have been flying around on Earth for a staggering 350 million years. The power of flight has helped them escape their enemies and travel to new areas to find food. Most flying insects have two pairs of wings, but different species have various wing shapes. The way they fly varies, too, so you can identify some insects by their flight patterns. For example, butterflies have two pairs of large, triangular wings which they flap slowly as they flutter here and there. Bees and wasps have narrower wings and fly a straighter path. Midges have narrow, transparent wings with long fringes. These tiny insects seem to dance as they hover in the air. The buzzing sound many insects make as they fly is the sound of their wings beating. Insects' wings are made of chitin, the same hard material as the rest of the body case. Veins fan out across the fragile wings to strengthen them. When they are not flying, many insects fold their wings away. They must protect them, because wings that are damaged or broken will not grow back.

Linked wings
A butterfly's front and rear wings overlap to make a single surface. Although they flap their wings quite slowly, butterflies are strong fliers.

Moths have special bristles on their rear wings that act as hooks to link the wings together. In flight, a bristle locks under a tiny catch on the front wing. You can see the dark bristle under the light-colored catch in this picture (left) of a buff ermine moth's wing.

Beetles' wings in flight
As a cockchafer prepares for takeoff, its wing cases lift up and the flying wings unfold. In flight, the wing cases are spread out and help keep the insect airborne.

Beetles' wings at rest
Cockchafers and other beetles have hard wing cases instead of true front wings. When the insect is resting, the hard cases cover and protect the thin flying wings underneath.

FACT BOX

• Dragonflies are among the oldest and most primitive types of insects. Their two pairs of wings beat independently but cannot be folded.

• Flying insects that have developed more recently, such as bees, wasps, and moths, have two pairs of wings that beat together and can be folded away.

• Mosquitoes can flap their wings up and down three hundred times per second.

How insects fly
Insects have no muscles in their wings to move them up and down. The wings are hinged to the insect's thorax and move up and down as the thorax changes shape. As the roof of the thorax is pulled down, the wings move up. As the front and rear ends of the thorax are pulled in, the wings move down.

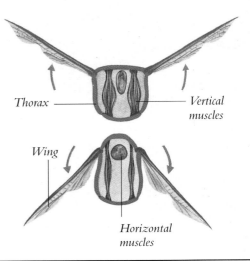

Thorax — *Vertical muscles*

Wing — *Horizontal muscles*

MIGRATION

Most insects spend their whole lives in one place. Others make long seasonal journeys, called migrations. They fly hundreds of miles to a different area and back again each year. Other kinds of animals migrate, too, including many species of birds. Most insects migrate to avoid cold weather or to find food for themselves or their young. A few insects, such as bogong moths in Australia, migrate to cooler areas to avoid the fierce summer heat and drought. Over two hundred types of butterflies and many kinds of moths migrate. These insects find their way by instinct, following the sun's path as it moves across the sky. Most fly and feed by day and rest at night. Migrating insects have traveled the same routes for centuries. They come and go at regular times each year. Other insects make irregular journeys, called irruptions. These flights are triggered by hunger when food is scarce.

Painted lady butterfly

The painted lady is found in many parts of the world. These colorful butterflies make long annual migrations. Painted ladies that hatch in Africa travel north to Europe in spring, and their offspring travel back to Africa in autumn.

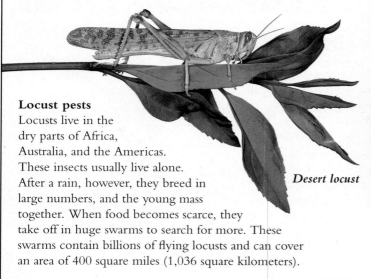

Desert locust

Locust pests
Locusts live in the dry parts of Africa, Australia, and the Americas. These insects usually live alone. After a rain, however, they breed in large numbers, and the young mass together. When food becomes scarce, they take off in huge swarms to search for more. These swarms contain billions of flying locusts and can cover an area of 400 square miles (1,036 square kilometers).

A swarm of locusts
These locusts *(above)* are descending on a farmer's field. Within minutes, they will eat all the crops and move on. A swarm might stay together several years.

Long-distance champions

The monarch butterfly *(below)* is a champion migrant. Monarchs starting out from southern hibernation sites in the spring lay eggs as they travel north. Their offspring reach Canada, completing the round-trip of over 3,700 miles (5,950 km) started by their ancestors.

In September, monarch butterflies (above) *head southward across the United States. Their flight looks fluttery and aimless, but monarchs fly at a steady 6 miles (10 km) per hour and cover up to 80 miles (129 km) a day.*

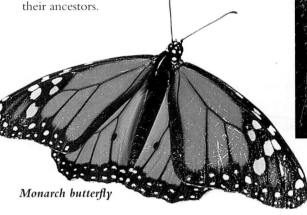

Monarch butterfly

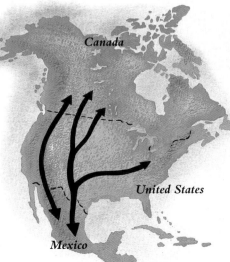

Migration map

This map shows the migration path of monarch butterflies. In late autumn, they arrive in Florida on the East Coast of the United States, in California on the West Coast, or in Mexico. There, they gather on trees to pass the winter. In March, they begin their journey north, lay their eggs, and die. When the eggs hatch, the cycle begins again. Newly hatched butterflies either continue north or return south, depending on the season.

FACT BOX

• Desert locusts are usually green in color, but when they swarm, their color changes. As they cluster together, they touch one another, triggering a chemical reaction that changes their body color to yellow, red, or black.

• In Australia, bogong moth caterpillars hatch in the southeastern lowlands in spring. In summer, the lowlands heat up, and the adult moths migrate to the Australian Alps, where it is cooler. There, they hibernate in crevices in the rocks until autumn, when it is cool enough to fly back to the lowlands.

FEEDING

INSECTS eat all kinds of different foods. About half of all insect species feed on plants. Others prey on animals, including other insects. Fleas and mosquitoes feed on the blood of birds and mammals. Many species eat both animals and plants. Some insects eat things we do not think of as food, including cloth, paper, cork, glue, wood, and feathers. Larvae, such as caterpillars and grubs, often have a completely different diet from their parents. Some insects are parasites — they live and feed on the bodies of other animals. Other insects are scavengers, feeding on dead animals and other decaying matter, such as droppings. Insects feed in two main ways. They either bite and munch on solid food, or suck the juices from plants or other animals. Insects' mouthparts are adapted to deal with their particular type of food. Those that bite and chew their food have cutting jaws. Insects that suck juices for food have mouthparts that form a hollow tube.

A tau emperor moth caterpillar (above) hangs upside down to munch through a tasty leaf. It begins by eating the edges of the leaf, then moves on to the juicy parts near the stem.

Biting jaws

Insects, such as ants, munch their food with mouthparts that have three pairs of jaws. The large jaws, called mandibles, are used to cut up food. Smaller jaws, called maxillae, push food into the mouth. A third pair of jaws forms the insect's lower lip.

Mandible

Ant

Harpoon jaws

This dragonfly nymph *(above)* has caught a small fish, called a stickleback. A dragonfly nymph has a special mouth for catching prey. Part of it, when not in use, is folded under the insect's head. In use, it shoots out suddenly to grab prey with pincerlike claws, then it draws the prey back to be eaten.

Sucking nectar

The mouthparts of butterflies and moths form a long, hollow tube, called a proboscis. Butterflies and moths feed on nectar, a sugary liquid found in flowers. The proboscis is used to suck in nectar as with a straw. When not in use, it is coiled up below the head.

Large skipper butterfly

Deadly assassin

The assassin bug preys on other insects, such as ladybugs. It injects its victims with a digestive liquid that paralyzes the insect and dissolves its body. When the insect's organs are dissolved, the assassin bug sucks out the juices until the body case is empty.

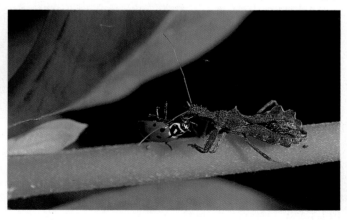

Piercing mouthparts

Mosquitoes feed on the blood of birds and mammals. They puncture their victim's skin with mouthparts like fine needles, called stylets. Then they suck up blood through a hollow tube. To stop the victim's blood from clotting, they pump their saliva into it.

SIGNS OF FEEDING

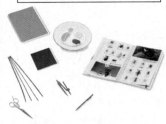

You will need: compass, stiff cardboard, scissors, pencil, 4 garden sticks, small samples of food (such as jam, meat, cheese, and fruit), notebook, field guide.

As insects eat, they leave damaged plants and other signs of feeding. Sometimes these signs are easier to spot than the insects themselves. Choose a small area, such as a fallen log, a bush, or a group of plants. Hundreds of insects will be nearby, but most are small and wary. Look along cracks or crevices in the bark, where insects might be hiding. Look under leaves and flowers. Any curled-up leaves could be an insect's home. Most plant-eating insects prefer one particular food and might eat only a part of that food plant. You will find butterflies and bees on flowers, drinking the sugary nectar. Caterpillars gather and feed on leaves. Aphids live on the stems of plants and suck out the sap. Find out if insects prefer certain foods by watching which ones visit different food samples.

Food samples

1 Use a compass to make four cardboard circles. Cut out the circles. Using the point of the compass or a sharp pencil, make a hole in the center of each circle. Push a garden stick through each hole. The cardboard circles should stay in position on the stick.

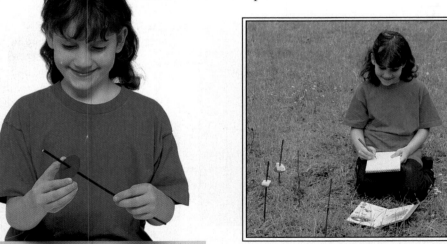

2 Outside, push the sticks into the ground and place food samples on the cardboard circles. Which foods do insects visit most? Do more insects visit at certain times of the day? Record your findings in a notebook.

Finding signs of feeding

1 In spring and summer, check the leaves of plants and trees for signs of insects feeding. Use a magnifying glass to take a close look and make notes of what you find.

2 Some insect larvae strip plants bare and nibble through stems. Others leave big ragged holes in leaves. A field guide can help you identify the larvae eating the plants.

3 Aphids and other bugs leave brown or yellow lines on crops when they suck out the sap. Aphids can also be found on the stems of roses.

M A T E R I A L S

You will need: magnifying glass, pencil, notebook, field guide.

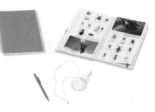

4 Many insects tunnel into wood. The lines on this tree trunk *(above)* were made by bark beetle larvae chewing their way between the bark and the wood underneath.

5 Look for white or brown markings on fresh leaves. Hold a leaf up to the light. Can you see any larvae inside? These larvae are called leaf miners. They tunnel inside the leaf and eat its tissue. Some eat patches of leaf, while others leave a winding trail.

INSECTS AND PLANTS

MANY insects depend on plants, but many plants depend on insects, too. To make seeds, a plant must be fertilized by pollen from the same plant or another of its species. Insects help by carrying pollen from one plant to another. Bees and butterflies visit flowers to feed on sugary nectar. They are attracted by the flowers' bright colors and sweet scents. As an insect sucks nectar, some of the flower's pollen clings to the insect's body. When the insect visits another flower, the pollen rubs off to pollinate and fertilize the plant. Many plants pollinated by butterflies have pink, red, or orange flowers, which are the colors butterflies see well. Some flowers have special markings, called nectar guides, radiating from the base of their petals. Some nectar guides show up only in ultraviolet light, but the eyes of insects, such as bees, are sensitive to ultraviolet light and can follow the guides to find the nectar in the middle of the flower.

In normal light (above), the evening primrose has yellow petals. In ultraviolet light (left), the flower's nectar guides show up as a dark patch that leads insects to the nectar in the flower's center.

Bumblebee

Insect pollination
When a bumblebee visits a flower, it sucks the flower's nectar with its long tongue and gathers pollen to feed the larvae in its nest. As the bee reaches into the center of the flower, pollen from the flower's stamens (male parts) rubs off on the bee's hairy body, coating it with dusty pollen grains.

After visiting the flower, the bee combs the pollen grains from its body with its legs, gathering grains into tiny pockets on its back legs. Some pollen, however, stays on the bee's body. When the bee visits the next flower, the pollen rubs off onto the stigmas (female parts) of that flower and fertilizes the plant.

Plants under attack

Aphids and their young *(left)* feed on plant stems. They pierce the outer layer of a stem with their mouthparts and suck up the sap. Plants make sap in their leaves as food for themselves, but the sap is also food for many insects.

Venus's-flytrap

Plants bite back

The Venus's-flytrap *(left)* has paired leaves with sharp spines on the edges. When an insect lands on the open leaves, the leaves snap shut, trapping the insect inside. Chemicals in the leaves slowly dissolve the insect's body, and the plant absorbs nutritious minerals from the insect.

Pitcher plants (above) *have pitcher-shaped leaves with slippery sides. An insect landing on the rim slips down inside the pitcher, falls into the liquid at the bottom, and drowns. The plant then absorbs nutrients from the insect's body.*

WOODLAND INSECTS

You will need:
old white sheet, collecting jar,
paintbrush, magnifying glass,
field guide, notebook, pencil,
colored pencils.

WOODS are great places to go insect-watching, but be sure you always take an adult with you. Woodland trees offer plenty of food, as well as shelter from winds and weather, so they are an ideal habitat for literally millions of insects. The number of insects you find will depend on the season. In spring, wildflowers blooming under the trees attract insects; in summer, the woods offer insects sunny clearings and cool shade. You can find a wide variety of insects in the woods. Large trees, such as oak and beech, are home to hundreds of different species. Choose a large tree and look at all of its parts — leaves, twigs, fruits or blossoms, bark, and roots — or make a survey of all the insects you can find on a single branch. Then, make a tree trap to catch insects that are active at night.

Woodland
insect chart

Studying life on a branch

1 Spread out a white sheet beneath a branch. Shake the branch to dislodge insects onto the sheet. If the branch is high, tap it with a stick, but be sure not to damage the tree.

2 Sweep the insects that drop onto the sheet into a collecting jar for study. Use a paintbrush to transfer the insects from the sheet to the jar without harming them.

3 Use a magnifying glass and a field guide to identify the insects. Then, release them and survey other trees. Make a chart to show the insect species found on each tree.

Make a tree trap

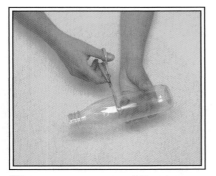

1 Use scissors to carefully cut a small plastic bottle in half. Have an adult help you.

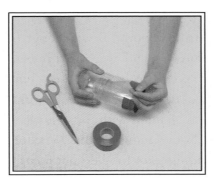

2 Push the neck of the bottle inside the bottom half and tape the two halves together to form the trap.

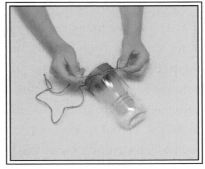

3 Loop a long piece of string around the open end of the trap and tie it securely with a knot. Bait the trap with a small piece of ham.

4 Tie the trap along a tree branch or hanging down underneath a branch. Leave the trap out overnight.

MATERIALS

You will need: scissors, small plastic bottle, strong tape, long piece of string, small piece of ham, magnifying glass, field guide, notebook, pencil.

5 Go back the next morning to check the trap. Use a magnifying glass and a field guide to identify the insects you have caught. Record your findings in a notebook. Carefully release the insects after you identify them.

COLOR AND CAMOUFLAGE

Insects have many enemies in the natural world. A wide range of animals, such as bats, frogs, lizards, birds, mammals, and even other insects eat them. Most adult insects try to escape predators by flying away, but not being seen at all is even better. Many insects have special colors and patterns on their bodies that help them blend in with the natural world, so predators do not see them. Some mimic a natural feature, such as a thorn or a twig. Predators hunting for food do not focus on their surroundings, so an insect that looks like a twig will not be noticed. These natural disguises are known as camouflage. Different kinds of insects imitate a wide range of natural objects. Some look like leaves, seeds, or flowers; others resemble moss, bark, lichen, sticks, or stones. Camouflage helps insects hide from danger. It also helps insects that hunt other creatures creep up unnoticed on their prey.

The toad grasshopper (above) lives in dry parts of Africa. Its body shape and coloring help it blend in with the bare rocks and stones of its habitat.

Hidden hunter

Can you see the mantis in this picture *(right)*? It is so well camouflaged that it is hard to spot against the bark. Mantises are predators that hunt other animals for food. This disguise helps them approach their prey unseen.

FACT BOX

• Red, yellow, and orange colors in insects are usually caused by chemicals left over from the insects' food.

• Caterpillars are particularly at risk from predators because they cannot fly away. Camouflage helps many of them stay hidden.

Changing camouflage

Peppered moths usually have whitish wings and bodies with black speckles *(right, upper)*. This coloring helps them blend in with tree bark. During the 1800s, however, many trees near towns were blackened with factory soot. Over the years, a darker variety of peppered moth *(right, lower)* became common in towns, because it blended in better with the sooty surroundings.

In its dormant state, the pupa of a swallowtail butterfly (right) *is very vulnerable to attack from predators. The pupa's skin is colored to blend in with the plant stem to which it is attached. Camouflage keeps the insect safe while it changes into a butterfly.*

Leaf mimic

The bush katydid *(above)* is from West Africa. The color, shape, and patterns of its wings help it mimic the leaves of its rain forest home. It even has lines that look like leaf veins on its wings, which makes the katydid very difficult to recognize among the leaves.

Acting like a twig

The waved umber moth caterpillar *(above)* is camouflaged to look like a twig. To complete its disguise, it holds its body at an angle on the branch. In this position, it looks just like a twig branching from the main stem. When danger threatens, the caterpillar keeps absolutely still.

WARNINGS AND DISGUISES

Bull's-eye moth

S OME kinds of insects are armed with poisonous stings or bites. Others have poisonous or foul-tasting fluids in their bodies. These kinds of insects do not have to hide from predators. Instead, they make themselves quite obvious. Their bodies have special warning colors that are used and understood throughout the animal world. Warning colors are often bright red or yellow, with black spots or stripes, which are patterns easily seen by predators. Ladybugs, for example, have bright red wing cases patterned with black spots. When an animal tries to eat a ladybug, the ladybug produces a foul-tasting fluid. Predators that have tried once will not try again — they will recognize the colors and avoid ladybugs in the future. Other insects take advantage of warning colors. Their bodies have the same colors as a poisonous species, but they are not poisonous and cannot sting or bite. Fungus beetles are red with black spots, just like ladybugs. They are harmless, but because they look like ladybugs, predators leave them alone.

Eyespots
The bull's-eye moth has two large eyespots on its rear wings. When the wings are open, the spots look like the eyes of a much larger animal, and they scare off predators.

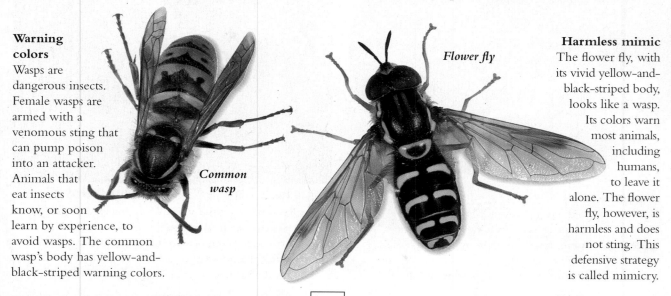

Warning colors
Wasps are dangerous insects. Female wasps are armed with a venomous sting that can pump poison into an attacker. Animals that eat insects know, or soon learn by experience, to avoid wasps. The common wasp's body has yellow-and-black-striped warning colors.

Common wasp

Flower fly

Harmless mimic
The flower fly, with its vivid yellow-and-black-striped body, looks like a wasp. Its colors warn most animals, including humans, to leave it alone. The flower fly, however, is harmless and does not sting. This defensive strategy is called mimicry.

Startle colors

Resting on a tree trunk with its wings closed, this moth (*left*) is well camouflaged against the bark. If, however, a predator comes too close, it spreads its front wings (*right*) to show its colorful rear wings. The bright flash of color can startle the hunter and distract it for a moment. Meanwhile, the moth flies to a new perch and closes its wings, becoming invisible again. The use of color to startle predators is quite common among insects and is a useful means of stalling a potential attacker for a few precious seconds.

A threatening display

The weta *(below)* is a large, rare insect from New Zealand. When startled, it raises its large, toothed hind legs above its head. Many creatures are frightened away by this menacing sight. Those creatures not scared off might get a painful kick from the weta's powerful legs.

The chrysalis of the black hairstreak butterfly (above) *looks just like the bird dropping to its left. Since birds will not taste their own droppings when searching for food, they leave the hairstreak alone. Looking like something inedible is a clever way to hide from predators, especially if you cannot fly.*

NATURE DETECTIVES

You will need: scissors, light green and dark green paper, 2 cardboard boxes, tape, paintbrush, paper towels, ivy leaves, cheesecloth, modeling clay, notebook, colored pencils.

SOME insects, such as walkingsticks, use camouflage to hide from predators. For an insect's camouflage to work, the insect must hide against the right color or kind of background. If it moves to a different place, it might become obvious to predators and open to attack. Walkingsticks are experts at disguise. Their long, slender bodies and sticklike legs make them very hard to see among twigs and leaves. You can experiment to see if they are also able to change their body color to match their surroundings. Sometimes you can buy walkingsticks at a pet store, or you can search for them by carefully looking at the leaves and twigs of plants in woodlands and city parks. Be sure to notice what walkingsticks feed on so you can give them the proper food.

Walkingsticks (above) *stay very still during the day. They usually move and feed at night.*

Color change test

1 Cut pieces of colored paper to line the insides of two cardboard boxes. Line one box with light green paper and the other with dark green paper. Attach the paper with tape.

2 Use a paintbrush to put some walkingsticks into the light green box. Add damp paper towels and leaves. Cover the box with cheesecloth weighted at the corners with clay.

3 Leave the box in a well-lit place for a day. Then look at the insects and use colored pencils to record their color. Transfer the insects to the dark green box. After another day, check them to see if they have changed color.

Raising walkingsticks

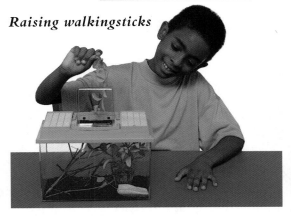

You will need: small tank (or large empty jar), soil, sticks, glass of water, ivy leaves, paper towels.

1 You can raise walkingsticks in a tank, or a large jar, that has a tight-fitting lid with small air holes. Put a layer of soil in the bottom and add some sticks and a glass of water containing the kind of leaves your walkingstick eats.

2 Put wet paper towels in a corner of the tank so the insects have enough moisture. Replace the towels regularly. Ask at the pet shop if the insects will need anything else.

Insect home

Would you recognize this object *(above)* as an insect's home? It is a gall called a robin's pincushion. A gall is a swelling on a plant caused by an insect. This gall was formed by a tiny wasp that laid its eggs on a rosebud. The gall contains many developing wasp larvae.

Hiding place

The nymph of a froghopper bug *(left)* protects itself from hungry enemies by producing a blob of unpleasant-looking foam. The foam is a common sight on plants. The nymph is usually hidden in the middle of the foam, where it can safely suck the plant's sap.

ATTACK AND DEFENSE

Puss moth caterpillar

INSECTS that feed on living animals, including other insects, must be able to hunt and catch their prey. They must also have a way to overpower their victims. Insects see movement well but have some difficulty spotting objects that are completely still. Some hunting insects take advantage of this weakness. They lie in wait for another insect to pass by, then spring out at it when it comes close. Many predators are well camouflaged and can hunt without being seen. If they keep very still, their victims will not notice them until it is too late. Some insects catch their prey by seizing them in powerful jaws; others use sharp spines on their legs. Some are armed with stings or poisons that can be used either for attack or for defense. Wasps and ants have venomous stings or bites that they use to overcome prey. Insects defend themselves, too, in various ways, often wounding their attackers. Some have poisonous bodies or taste horrible; others have sharp spines or can squirt stinging liquid.

The puss moth caterpillar has several lines of defense if it is threatened. The caterpillar rears its head to reveal a bright red frill and large black eyespots. At the same time, it waves its tail, which looks like a snake's forked tongue. If the enemy is still not scared away, it squirts stinging acid out of a gland in its thorax.

FACT BOX

• The pupa of the South African leaf beetle contains a powerful poison that bushmen use on the tips of their arrows when hunting. If an arrow so much as grazes an animal's body, the animal will die.

• When it is threatened, the bombardier beetle mixes two chemicals in its abdomen, producing a small explosion and a blast of hot gases that shoots out of the insect's rear end.

Prickly meal
Caterpillars are a juicy meal for predators, such as birds and lizards. Some species, such as the emperor moth caterpillar, have sharp, spiny bristles on their bodies for protection. When the spines prick the predator's mouth, it drops the caterpillar.

Emperor moth caterpillar

Stinging weapons

This sand-tailed digger wasp *(left)* is holding a weevil it has paralyzed with its sting. Many wasp species use poison to capture prey. The stinger is a modified ovipositor, which is the organ used to lay eggs. Therefore, only female wasps can sting.

The barbed spine of a wasp's stinger is connected to a poison sac, which pumps poison into the wound.

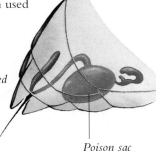

Stinger

Poison sac

Group attack

These ants *(above)* are working together to attack a large insect. By working as a group, the ants are able to kill and carry away prey that is much larger than what they might be able to handle individually.

Hidden hunters

The praying mantis *(above)* is camouflaged to look like the plant on which it lives. It hunts by keeping very still; only its eyes swivel as it scans for victims. When an insect lands nearby, the mantis darts forward with lightning speed and grabs the victim in its front legs. The sharp spines on its legs keep a firm grip while the mantis eats its prey alive.

WASPS AND BEES

People have collected honey for many centuries. They keep bees in hives so they can harvest the honey easily. To gather honey, a beekeeper (above) removes part of a hive. The beekeeper's heavy clothing protects against stings.

Wasps and bees belong to the insect order Hymenoptera. There are thousands of different kinds, and they live in almost every part of the world. Many kinds of wasps and bees have yellow and black warning colors, and many have stingers. Most are solitary insects that live alone, but bumblebees, honeybees, and social wasps live in large groups, called colonies. Honeybees nest in trees or in beehives. The colony has a single queen, hundreds of drones, and thousands of worker bees. The queen is the largest bee. Her task is to lay eggs. The drones are male bees. Their job is to mate with the queen, so she can lay eggs. The workers are undeveloped female bees. They do all the work of the colony, including building and repairing the nest and bringing nectar and pollen from flowers to the nest. The workers also feed the larvae, or grubs, with pollen and honey. In a few weeks, the grubs become pupae, and then adult bees. All bees and wasps go through complete metamorphosis to become adults.

Bees make honey to feed their larvae and to keep themselves alive in winter.

Inside the hive
Worker honeybees *(left)* build six-sided cells from beeswax on sheets called combs. Some of these cells are filled with honey and pollen; others contain eggs or developing larvae.

Bee dance
When a bee finds a source of nectar, it tells other bees about it by doing a special dance, such as a figure-eight dance. The angle of the bee's body tells the other bees the direction of the food. If the nectar is close by, the bee energetically waggles its body.

You might see wasps on a fence post gathering wood, because common wasps build nests of paper. They make the paper by chewing up wood fibers. If you notice a wooden post with tiny, parallel grooves, the grooves might have been made by a wasp collecting fibers.

FACT BOX

• In the 1800s, it was fashionable for ladies to have narrow waists like wasps. The "wasp waist" was created by wearing a tight corset, which was very uncomfortable.

• Male orchid bees from South America make a perfume from orchid flowers to attract females.

• Paintings in Egyptian tombs prove that ancient Egyptians kept bees for honey 2,500 years ago.

Inside a wasp nest

This cutaway view of a wasp nest *(right)* shows how the outer layers of paper protect the cells in the middle. A single larva develops in each cell. Worker wasps build the combs, clean the cells, forage for food, and feed the grubs chewed-up insects.

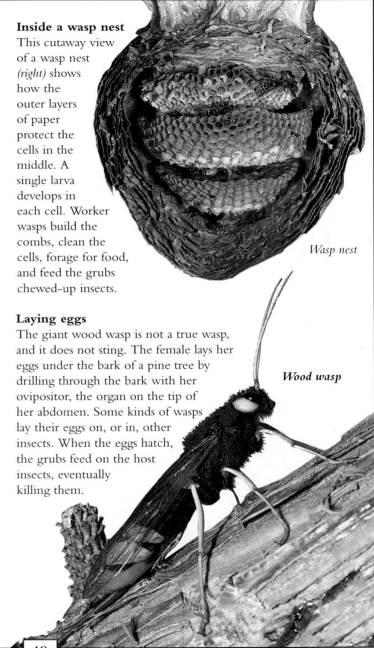

Wasp nest

Wood wasp

Laying eggs

The giant wood wasp is not a true wasp, and it does not sting. The female lays her eggs under the bark of a pine tree by drilling through the bark with her ovipositor, the organ on the tip of her abdomen. Some kinds of wasps lay their eggs on, or in, other insects. When the eggs hatch, the grubs feed on the host insects, eventually killing them.

ANTS AND TERMITES

Ant

An ant smells the air with its antennae. Ants cannot see very well, so smell and touch are vital senses. When ants meet, they touch antennae. Intruders with the wrong scent are driven away.

ANTS and termites belong to different insect orders, yet they behave in similar ways. They are social insects and live in colonies that might contain thousands, or even millions, of insects, each with its own role. Queen ants (there may be several in one nest) lay eggs. As in a beehive, the tasks of the colony are carried out by undeveloped females, called workers. Some ant species have workers with large jaws, called soldiers, that guard and defend the nest. In summer, winged male and female ants fly out of their nests to mate, and the females start new colonies. In termite colonies, the queen has a king that stays by her side to fertilize the eggs. Termite workers can be either male or female.

Black worker ants (above) carry the pupae to safety when their nest has been disturbed. In the nest, the workers feed, tend, and clean the larvae.

Gathering food

In South America, leafcutter ants bite off large pieces of leaf. Their powerful jaws slice through the leaves like scissors. Then each ant carries a piece of leaf bigger than itself back to the nest. The leaves are used to grow a special fungus the ants feed on.

Leafcutter ants

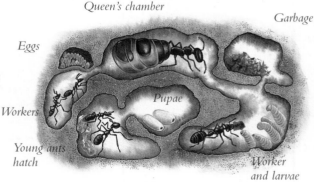

Queen's chamber

Garbage

Eggs

Workers

Pupae

Young ants hatch

Worker and larvae

Inside an ant nest

Ant nests are usually underground and have many chambers, or rooms, and passages. Different chambers contain the eggs, the larvae, the pupae, and the queen. Other chambers contain food or garbage. Worker ants adjust the temperature of the nest by opening or closing passages.

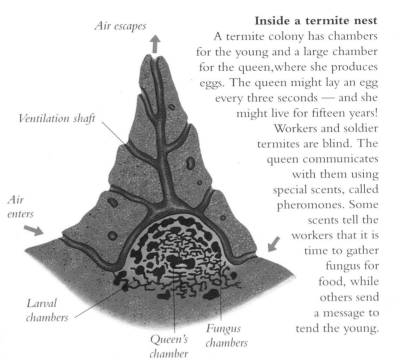

Inside a termite nest

A termite colony has chambers for the young and a large chamber for the queen, where she produces eggs. The queen might lay an egg every three seconds — and she might live for fifteen years! Workers and soldier termites are blind. The queen communicates with them using special scents, called pheromones. Some scents tell the workers that it is time to gather fungus for food, while others send a message to tend the young.

Ventilation shaft

Air enters

Larval chambers

Queen's chamber

Fungus chambers

Towering home

A few kinds of termites build spectacular termite mounds like this one *(above)* in Africa. Underground nests have tall towers, made of soil, that rise high into the air. Above the chambers, these towers have ventilation shafts that circulate the air inside the nest to keep it cool.

Workers and soldiers

Termites *(right)* live in warm grasslands all over the world. They feed mostly on plant matter and do a valuable job in recycling nutrients back into the soil. Worker termites are wingless. Soldier termites have large, armored heads. Their job is to defend the nest.

INVESTIGATING ANTS

*You will need:
gardening gloves, peeled
ripe fruit, piece of paper,
magnifying glass.*

An ant colony is like an underground city, and each citizen has a particular job to do. Workers scurry back and forth, scouting for food and bringing it to the nest. When the nest is disturbed, the ants swarm to defend their home. The key to the smooth running of the colony is good communication. Ants communicate mainly through touch and by using powerful scents, called pheromones. Different scents tell worker ants that the larvae must be cleaned or fed, or that the nest should be repaired. When an ant finds a new source of food, it hurries back to the nest. As it runs along, it presses its body against the ground, leaving a trail of scent that other ants can follow. You can watch ants communicating this way by putting down some food near an ant nest. An even better way to study ants, however, is to start a colony. You can establish an ant colony in a glass jar covered with dark paper. If you remove the paper covering after a few days, you will see ant tunnels.

Watching ant trails

1 Wearing gloves, find a trail of ants. Follow the trail to see where the ants are going. Does the trail lead to food? Does it lead to the ant nest?

2 Put peeled, ripe fruit down on a piece of paper near the ant trail. (The paper makes it easier to see the ants.) Watch what happens when the workers find the fruit.

3 Once an ant has laid a scent trail to the fruit, other ants follow. Move the fruit to another part of the paper. What happens? Do the ants go straight to the new food site?

Start an ant colony

1 Cut a piece of dark paper large enough to fit around the jar. Tape the paper in position.

2 Wearing gloves, use a trowel to almost fill the jar with garden soil. Put leaves on top of the soil.

3 Use a paintbrush to capture some ants in a collecting jar. Transfer the ants to the large jar.

MATERIALS

You will need: dark-colored paper, large jar, scissors, tape, gardening gloves, trowel, garden soil, leaves, paintbrush, collecting jar, ripe fruit or jam, paper towels, cheesecloth.

If you have captured a queen, you might see workers tending eggs or larvae in special chambers.

4 Feed the ants with pieces of ripe fruit or some jam. Add damp paper towels to provide moisture. Feed the ants daily, and refresh the leaves and damp towels regularly.

5 Cover the top of the jar with a piece of cheesecloth, so the ants cannot escape. Secure the cheesecloth with tape. Keep the ant colony in a cool place.

6 After a few days, remove the dark paper to view the colony. You should see winding tunnels built against the sides of the jar.

BEAUTIFUL BUTTERFLIES

Light bouncing off tiny ridges on the overlapping scales of a morpho butterfly's wing produces an intense blue color, as seen in this close-up (above).

BUTTERFLY wings are covered with thousands of tiny, overlapping scales. The scales are brightly colored, or they reflect light in a way that makes them shine with color. The natural beauty of butterflies has made them a target of collectors for hundreds of years. The survival of some species is now threatened by the activities of collectors. Some butterflies are in danger of dying out, also, because their habitats are being cleared or drained for farmland or to make room to build houses. Some kinds of butterflies have wings with warning colors that let predators know they are poisonous to eat. Poisonous butterflies of different species in the same area sometimes look identical, which strengthens the warning message sent to predators. Other butterflies are harmless but mimic poisonous species. Their colors fool predators into avoiding them as well. All butterflies go through complete metamorphosis, changing from caterpillars to pupae before becoming adults.

Painted lady butterfly

Swallowtail butterfly

At rest

Like most butterflies, the painted lady rests with its wings closed. The undersides of its colorful wings are dull, which helps conceal the butterfly from predators when it lands.

Club antennae
It is difficult to tell a butterfly from a moth, but a good guide is to look at the antennae. The swallowtail butterfly, like most butterflies, has antennae with clubbed tips. Moths' antennae vary a great deal, but most are straight or feathered.

Males and females

The colors and patterns on their wings help butterflies recognize others of their species. Males and females often have slightly different markings, so they can identify each other for mating. For example, only male orange tip butterflies *(right)* have orange tips on their wings. Females of this species *(left)* have gray wing tips.

Viceroy butterfly

Monarch butterfly

Winter sleep

Butterflies cannot stay active in cold weather. Some find a safe, sheltered spot for the winter and hibernate. This peacock butterfly *(below)* is hibernating on a tree trunk. The dark undersides of its wings help conceal it in dark corners.

Copycat colors

These two butterflies *(above)* look very similar, but they belong to two different species. Monarch butterflies are poisonous. Their caterpillars feed on poisonous milkweed plants and store the poison in their bodies. The viceroy butterfly looks just like the monarch, but it is harmless. Birds and reptiles see the warning colors and do not try to eat it.

BUTTERFLY GARDEN

MATERIALS

You will need: gardening gloves, window box or large tub, garden soil, packet of wildflower seeds, watering can, notebook, pencil, field guide.

THE best way to attract butterflies is to plant a butterfly garden. You can make a small garden in a window box, or a larger one in the yard with room for many different plants and herbs. Choose plants that bloom at various times of the year. Different plants attract certain butterflies and their larvae. Caterpillars feed on leafy plants, such as grasses, thistles, and nettles. Adult moths and butterflies gather on plants with nectar-bearing flowers, such as wallflowers, buddleia, goldenrod, candytuft, and ice plants. Moths are attracted to honeysuckle because the flowers release a sweet smell at night. Ask an adult's permission before planting the garden. Also, try not to use insecticides in the garden. In a small space, such as a window box, you could plant verbena, phlox, and alyssum. You could also grow herbs, such as marjoram and thyme. When studying butterflies, keep very still and do not let your shadow fall over them, or you will frighten them.

Plant a window box

3 Keep the soil moist. Seedlings will sprout in a few weeks. As the plants grow, water them regularly and note the kinds of insects they attract.

1 Wearing gloves, fill about three-quarters of a window box or a large tub with garden soil.

2 Scatter wildflower seeds on the soil. Do *not* dig up wild plants. Cover the seeds with more soil.

Plant a butterfly garden

1 In spring, grow plants from seeds or buy young plants. Wearing gloves, use a trowel to dig up a patch of soil.

2 Break up any large clods of earth with a rake. Then rake over the top of the soil to spread it out evenly.

3 With the trowel, dig small holes for your plants. Place the plants in the holes and press the soil down firmly around them.

MATERIALS

You will need: packets of seeds or young plants, gardening gloves, trowel, rake, watering can, notebook, pencil, field guide.

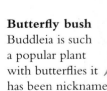

4 Water the plants well and keep watering them on a regular basis throughout the spring and summer. Water plants in the morning; midday sun might scorch wet leaves.

5 Watch to see which butterflies visit your flowers. A field guide can help you identify them. Note which species prefer which flowers and which plant is the most popular.

Butterfly bush
Buddleia is such a popular plant with butterflies it has been nicknamed "butterfly bush." Butterflies, such as small tortoiseshells (*above*), peacocks, painted ladies, commas, and red admirals, are attracted to buddleia's masses of sweet-smelling mauve or purple flowers.

INSECTS OF THE NIGHT

Most insects are active only by day and rest at night, but some hunt and feed in darkness, or at dawn and dusk. Animals that are active at night are called nocturnal. Moths are closely related to butterflies, but, unlike butterflies, most are nocturnal. Moths and other nocturnal insects have senses suited to the darkness. They cannot communicate with other insects through color, since colors cannot be seen at night. So night-flying insects use other signals, especially smells and sounds. Some moths use pheromones, or powerful scents, to communicate with the opposite sex. Other insects, such as crickets and cicadas, send out sound signals to attract a mate. Moths are very successful insects. There are more than 100,000 kinds of moths compared to about 15,000 kinds of butterflies.

Signaling with light
Glowworms communicate with light. To attract a mate, a female glowworm *(above)* gives off a greenish light from her abdomen. The light is produced by a chemical reaction.

Mating song
The song of the cicada is a common sound in warm countries at dawn and dusk. This insect uses special muscles on its abdomen to produce a stream of high-pitched clicking sounds. Male cicadas sing to attract females. The songs of some cicadas can be heard over 500 yards (457 m) away.

A firefly (above) uses light to communicate. A male signals as it flies overhead, looking for a mate. When a female sees the signal, she flashes back. Each species of firefly has its own signal.

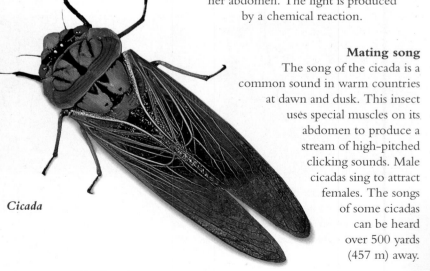

Cicada

Mighty moth

Not all moths are dull in color. The spectacular atlas moth has beautiful markings on its wings. The atlas moth is one of the largest species of moths. It can have a wingspan of almost 10 inches (25 cm). When a moth is at rest, it usually spreads its wings out on each side of its body. Most moths have stout, hairy bodies. Some have eyespots on their wings to confuse or scare off hungry predators.

Atlas moth

Tiger moth

Confusing clicks

Tiger moths have a unique way of foiling bats hunting at night. Bats hunt by echolocation, sending out a stream of high-pitched squeaks and clicks that bounce off their prey. The bats listen to the echoes to pinpoint the location of the prey. The tiger moth, however, can produce its own stream of clicks that jams the bat's echolocation and confuses the hunter.

Moth antennae

Moths often have large, feathery or fernlike antennae *(left)* that are very sensitive to smell. Female moths attract males by producing special scents. Some male moths have such sensitive antennae they can detect the scent released by a female up to 7 miles (11 km) away. When they are close to the female, they can compare the scents reaching each antenna to find her exact location.

MOTH WATCH

MATERIALS

You will need:
gardening gloves, trowel,
small flashlight, camera.

Mᴏᴛʜs, like all insects, are cold-blooded creatures. Most cold-blooded animals are active only during daylight hours, when sunlight can warm their bodies. So, how do moths get warm enough to fly at night? Some moths have furry bodies, which hold the heat the insects absorb during the day. Even so, they still have to warm up their muscles before they fly. They warm up by quivering their bodies and vibrating their wings before takeoff. These movements generate heat. Moths are attracted to bright lights, such as streetlights, and will fly toward them. So, when it is dark, you can attract moths to study by using light. Set up a flashlight in the ground and wait for the moths to arrive. If you have a camera, try photographing the moths illuminated by your flashlight. Another way to attract moths is with tasty food. Like butterflies, moths feed on liquid food, which they suck up with their proboscis, or tubelike tongue. A mixture of mashed fruit and sugar will bring them fluttering around.

Flashlight attraction

1 Wearing gloves, dig a small hole in the ground with a trowel. Do your digging in daylight, and be sure to ask an adult for permission.

2 At dusk, turn on a flashlight and put it in the hole you dug. Fill in the hole with soil to hold the flashlight in position.

3 Step back and watch the moths flutter around the light. Use a camera to take flash photographs of the moths.

A sweet moth feast

1 Spoon brown sugar into a measuring cup. You will need about 2 cups (400 grams) of sugar. Transfer the sugar to a mixing bowl.

2 Add overripe fruit and mash it with a fork. Keep mashing until the fruit becomes a pulp. Add warm water until the mixture is runny.

MATERIALS

You will need: spoon, brown sugar, measuring cup, mixing bowl, overripe fruit, fork, warm water, paintbrush, flashlight, field guide.

Moths find their way in darkness by using the moon as a guide. At night, moths and other insects often flutter around streetlights. They mistake streetlights for the moon and lose their sense of direction.

3 Paint the mixture onto a tree trunk or a fence post. When it is dark, return with a flashlight to watch the moths feeding. Use a field guide to identify the moths.

INSECT FRIENDS AND FOES

INSECTS are vital to life on Earth. They do many helpful jobs all across the planet. They pollinate flowers and provide food for larger creatures. They eat dead plants and animals, helping return nutrients to the soil. Silkworms and honeybees are so useful that they have been kept by humans for centuries. Some insects, however, do great harm. They do serious damage to crops, bringing hardship, and even starvation, to those areas. Fleas and cockroaches infest many homes. Termites and some beetles eat timber, destroying both living trees and buildings or furniture made of wood. Flying insects that feed on blood, such as mosquitoes, are some of the deadliest animals in the world. They pass on diseases, such as malaria, which can be fatal.

This fly (above) *is feeding on ham in a sandwich. Flies also feed on animal droppings and garbage. They transfer germs to our food with their feet and mouthparts.*

A nutritious food

In many parts of the world, people eat insects. They are a nutritious food that can be served in many different ways. This man *(left)* is selling fried grasshoppers at a stall in Uganda, in Africa. In Asia, stir-fried locusts are a delicacy. The diets of some aboriginal Australians include bogong moths and juicy grubs. People in Corsica and Sardinia enjoy a special cheese with maggots.

FACT BOX

• Cochineal insects from Central America are crushed to provide a red dye used to color food. The Aztecs used this method to color food six hundred years ago.

• In Africa, tsetse flies spread sleeping sickness, a deadly disease. In South America, assassin bugs transmit Chagas' disease, which can cause serious health problems.

Pest controller

Ladybugs *(above)* eat aphids and other sap-sucking bugs that attack plant stems. Some farmers release ladybugs onto their crops to control insect pests.

Crop eater

Colorado potato beetles *(left)* feed on potato plants. In the 1800s, these beetles caused great damage to potato crops in North America. Now, powerful chemicals, called insecticides, are used to kill these insects. The insecticides are sprayed onto crops from the air.

Silkworm farms

These silkworms *(above)* are about to spin cocoons and pupate. In many parts of Asia, silkworms are kept on farms. The caterpillars are fattened on the leaves of the mulberry tree. Silkworms living in the wild in China and India produce wild silk. Silk is the strongest natural fiber.

Silk maker

Some kinds of insect larvae spin a silken cocoon and pupate inside. Silk moth caterpillars, called silkworms, spin a strong, fine thread in a web around their bodies. The cocoons of some species are collected and the fibers unwound to make natural silk cloth. The holes in this cocoon *(right)* show that parasites have attacked it to prey on the pupa inside.

GLOSSARY

arachnid – an invertebrate similar to an insect, but with eight legs and no antennae, such as spiders and ticks.

camouflage – coloring, shape, or movement that hides something by making it blend in with its surroundings.

cerci – feelers on the back end of an insect's abdomen that are sensitive to vibrations caused by noise or movement.

chitin – the hard substance that forms the outer shell of an insect's body.

chrysalis – a protective casing that covers the pupa of an insect as it develops into its adult form; a cocoon.

Coleoptera – an order of insects, including beetles, with shell-like front wing covers that protect soft rear wings folded underneath.

coxa – the part of an insect's leg that connects it to the thorax.

crustacean – an animal with a segmented body, a hard exoskeleton, and two pairs of antennae. Some crustaceans, such as wood lice and water fleas, resemble insects.

Diptera – an order of insects, including flies and mosquitos, with transparent front wings and halteres, or balancing organs, instead of rear wings.

dormant – temporarily inactive; in a resting or sleeping state, usually for an extended period of time.

echolocation – a process that uses sound waves reflected by an object back to the sender to determine the location and distance of the object.

exoskeleton – the hard outer surface of an insect's body.

gall – a growth, or swelling, on plants caused by insect parasites, usually in the larva stage.

grub – a wormlike insect larva.

halteres – club-shaped organs used for balancing that insects, such as flies, have instead of rear wings.

Hemiptera – an order of insects, including various bugs, with front wings that have a hard, thick base but are soft at the tip.

Hymenoptera – an order of insects, including ants, bees, and wasps, with thin, stiff wings that interlock in flight.

invertebrate – an animal without a backbone.

irruption – a sudden and irregular migration of insects due to a lack of food in an area.

larva – the wingless, wormlike form of an insect in the stage of development between the egg and the pupa.

Lepidoptera – an order of insects, including butterflies and moths, with long antennae and four broad wings covered with overlapping scales that often are brightly colored.

mandibles – the large, powerful jaws of a chewing insect, used to cut, tear, and grind food.

maxillae – a second pair of jaws behind the mandibles of a chewing insect, used to push food down the throat.

metamorphosis – changing physical form in a series of stages, such as a caterpillar changing into a butterfly.

mimicry – the biological advantage of one insect looking like another, especially for protection against predators.

molt – to shed a covering, such as skin or a shell, at regular intervals of development before growing a new covering.

myriapod – an invertebrate similar to an insect, but with many body segments, each of which usually has legs, such as centipedes and millipedes.

nymph – the larva of an insect that closely resembles an adult of its species except for incomplete development of the wings and reproductive system.

ocelli – the simple eyes of an insect that are used to distinguish light and dark, as distinct from the compound eyes with which insects see fine details.

Orthoptera – an order of insects, including crickets and grasshoppers, with two pairs of straight wings — tough, narrow front wings and finer, broader rear wings.

ovipositor – the organ, at the tip of an insect's abdomen, that is used to lay eggs.

parasite – a plant or animal that lives in or on another plant or animal to get its food.

pheromone – a special, recognizable scent produced by an insect to attract and communicate with other insects of its species.

proboscis – the tubelike mouthpart of sucking insects, such as bees and butterflies.

prolegs – extra "false" legs found on the abdomen of some insect larvae, such as caterpillars, but not found on adult insects of that species.

pupa – the form of an insect in the middle stage of development when the larva is enclosed in a protective casing, such as a chrysalis, while it changes into an adult.

scavenger – an insect that feeds on decaying plants or animals or on animal droppings.

spiracle – one of many tiny openings along each side of an insect's body that lets air inside the body for breathing.

stylet – the needlelike mouthpart of a mosquito used to pierce its victim's skin, inject saliva into the wound, and sip out the thinned blood.

thorax – the middle section of an insect's body, between the head and the abdomen, to which the legs and wings are attached.

trachea – the tube attached to a spiracle that carries air entering through the spiracle to other parts of the insect's body.

BOOKS

Ants: A Great Community. Secrets of the Animal World (series). Andreu Llamas (Gareth Stevens)

Bees: Busy Honeymakers. Secrets of the Animal World (series). Eulalia García (Gareth Stevens)

Bizarre Insects. Weird and Wacky Science (series). Margaret J. Anderson (Enslow)

Bugs that Go Blam! and Other Creepy-Crawler Trivia. Barbara Seuling (Willowisp Press)

Butterflies: Magical Metamorphosis. Secrets of the Animal World (series). Eulalia García (Gareth Stevens)

Caterpillars, Bugs, and Butterflies. Young Naturalist Field Guides (series). Mel Boring (Gareth Stevens)

Cockroaches, Stinkbugs, and Other Creepy Crawlers. The Draw Science (series). Christine Becker (Lowell House)

Dangerous Insects. The Encyclopedia of Danger (series). Michel Preissel and Missy Allen (Chelsea House)

Flies Taste with Their Feet: Weird Facts about Insects. Strange World (series). Melvin Berger (Scholastic)

Flutter by, Butterfly. Nature Close-ups (series). Densey Clyne (Gareth Stevens)

Insects. Under the Microscope (series). John Woodward (Gareth Stevens)

Insects and Spiders. Discoveries (series). David Burnie (Time-Life)

VIDEOS

Ants and How They Live. (AIMS Multimedia)

Bee Basics. (Pyramid Film and Video)

The Benefits of Insects. (National Geographic Society)

The Chirping Crickets. (Environmental Media)

Insect Mouthparts. (Britannica Films)

The Insect Series: Collecting Butterflies and Moths. (Chip Taylor Communications)

WEB SITES

www.uky.edu/Agriculture/Entomology/ythfacts/entyouth.htm

insects.ummz.lsa.umich.edu/YES/YES.html

Some web sites stay current longer than others. For further web sites, use your search engines to locate the following topics: *ants, bees, beetles, bugs, butterflies, centipedes, entomology, flies, grasshoppers, insects,* and *moths.*

INDEX

PICTURE CREDITS

b=bottom, t=top, c=center, l=left, r=right

Heather Angel: 36t. Michael Chinery: 41bl. Bruce Coleman Ltd./J. Brackenbury: 22t /John Cancalosi: 8bl /Fogden: 59br /J. Grayson: 50tr /J. Murray: 62b /A. Purcell: 32br /Kim Taylor: 16t; 17tl; 25bl, r; 28bl; 36bl, r; 46b; 54bl. Ecoscene/G. Neden: 61bl /Robin Williams: 14bl. FLPA: 24bl; /R. Austing: 31tr /B. Borrell: 23c, 63tl /T. Davidson: 48br /P. Heard: 40t /Hosking: 43bl, 51tl /G. Hyde: 43br /B. Lea/Dembinsky: 37r /D. Maslowski: 44tr /K. Rushforth: 63bl /L. West: 33br, 55bl /A. Wharton: 31tl. Holt Studios/Nigel Cattlin: 12b, 14t, 41br. Nature Photographers Ltd/Nicholas Brown: 8t /Paul Sterry: 16b, 59bl. NHPA/S. Dalton: 58bl. Papillio Photographic 8br; 18t; 22br; 23br; 28t; 30t, br; 40b; 45bl, r; 48bl; 54t; 55tl, r; 58tr. Planet Earth Pictures/Nick Garbutt: 4bl /S. Hopkin: 62t /Steve Nicholls: 24br /D. Tackett: 47br. Tony Stone Worldwide: 5bl. Lucy Tizard: 48t, c. Warren Photographic/Jane Burton: 18bl, 42t; /Kim Taylor: 5br, 17bl, 18br, 33t, 47tl, 49tr, 51b, 55br. Zefa: 13br; 15b; 17tr, br; 19b; 22bl; 28br; 29tl, r; 33bl; 37tl, tl; 41tl; 43tr, l; 47bl; 49tl, b; 58br; 59t; 63tr.